Historic Interiors

Historic Interiors

of England, Wales, and Northern Ireland

A PHOTOGRAPHIC TOUR

Photographs by Andreas von Einsiedel

and Nadia Mackenzie

Text by Margaret Willes

Harry N. Abrams, Inc., Publishers

First published in Great Britain in 1999 by
National Trust Enterprises Ltd,
36 Queen Anne's Gate, London SW1H 9AS

Distributed in 1999 by Harry N. Abrams, Incorporated, New York

British Library Cataloguing in Publication Data
A catalogue record for this book is available from the British Library.

ISBN 0 7078 0350 0
ISBN 0-8109-6388-4 (Abrams)

Picture research by Margaret Willes

Edited by Helen Fewster
Designed and typeset in Carter Cone Galliard by Peter and Alison Guy
Production management by Bob Towell
Printed and bound in China
Phoenix Offset

Frontispiece: The hall at CASTLE WARD in County Down, built in the 1760s by Bernard
Ward, later 1st Viscount Bangor, and his wife, Lady Anne. He favoured classical architecture,
she Gothick, and the interior reflects their difference in tastes. In the hall, Bernard Ward's classical taste prevailed, with a screen of Doric columns made from scagliola, powdered marble.
[AVE]

Contents

Introduction

This book concentrates on the insides of houses. The reader has passed through the front door and stands poised to take a tour. But unlike the normal tour of a country house, the visitor travels through time as well as going round the building. The various 'chapters' or sections describe different parts of the house, from great halls to libraries and chapels, and in doing so, each section moves through the centuries.

This is a book of houses – not castles or monasteries – and of country houses, not town dwellings. Thus it starts with late medieval manor houses like Cotehele in Cornwall and Rufford Old Hall, Lancashire, and ends with Polesden Lacey, Surrey, where Mrs Greville was able to maintain a country-house style of living in the 1920s and 30s, when many others had given up the effort. The rooms are what are often described as rooms of promenade or public rooms, though bedrooms are included. The service quarters and nurseries are not – and bathrooms make a guest appearance in the bedroom chapter. The National Trust has recently published several books on the service and the 'downstairs' areas. One of my colleagues asked when the upstairs was going to get a look in – so here it is.

All the houses discussed here are owned by the National Trust, although there are references to other buildings as comparisons or important examples. It may be that some of your favourite National Trust houses are not included because I have concentrated on the work of two outstanding interior photographers, Nadia Mackenzie and Andreas von Einsiedel, for consistency of style. But I hope that regret at omissions will be redressed by the pleasure of discovering houses that are not familiar.

The earliest houses described here are laid out more or less on the E-plan, with a hall in the centre, flanked by wings containing the service quarters at one end, and the more private family rooms at the other. This layout made it well-nigh impossible to place the entrance in the centre of the main front. For builders and designers fuelled with the Renaissance enthusiasm for the symmetry of classical architecture this was something of a headache. Bess of Hardwick and her architect, Robert Smythson, ingeniously solved

Above and right: Two details of the plasterwork that decorates the hall at Castle Ward (*see frontispiece*). Following the medieval tradition of hanging armour and weapons in the hall, the plasterwork includes trophies of arms, but also of the chase and farm, and of musical instruments. Several of the motifs are the real thing – hats, baskets and violins – dipped in plaster. [AVE]

this in the 1590s by twisting the great hall at Hardwick Hall in Derbyshire around on its axis, but others were slow to follow suit.

When Charles II was restored to the English throne in 1660, he and his courtiers returned with ideas about planning and layout that they had seen during their years of exile on the Continent. The gentleman architect, Roger Pratt, who had travelled in France and Italy in the 1640s, designed Coleshill in Berkshire for his cousin Sir George. He dealt with the problem of symmetry by taking the living rooms – the parlour and great chamber – from one end of the hall and placing them in the centre of the building, behind a two-storeyed entrance hall. 'Let the fairest room above be placed in the very midst of the house, as the bulk of man is between the members', he declared.

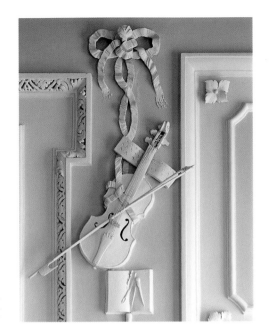

Pratt also recommended that the ground floor be raised and approached by a flight of steps to add height and majesty to the house, and to supply 'a very good story' below for the service quarters. This represented not merely an architectural revolution, but reflected a change in the style of the household. In previous centuries servants went all over the house, attending to the wishes of the master and his family. Now began the idea of separation between the upstairs and downstairs areas, with servants keeping to the basement area during the day, sleeping in the attic quarters by night, and attending to the intimate needs of their masters and mistresses by way of the backstairs.

This new style of living is succinctly shown in the superb, early eighteenth-century baby's house brought to Uppark, West Sussex, by Sarah Lethieullier when she married Sir Matthew Fetherston-haugh in 1746. This large-scale model was not a toy as such, but rather a means by which girls could learn how to run their own households. In the lowest level can be seen the kitchen and the housekeeper's room, with the rooms of promenade on the floor above, including a bedroom where the lady of the house has just given birth, and more bedrooms on the top level. The separation between family and servants is nicely shown by the different materials used for the dolls: wax for the family, wood for the servants.

For much of the eighteenth century, the Palladian style held sway – the tenets of the Roman architect Vitruvius as interpreted by the sixteenth-century Italian architect, Andreas Palladio. These principles can be clearly seen at Kedleston Hall in Derbyshire, the interior of which was laid out in the 1760s by Robert Adam for Sir Nathaniel Curzon. The main block of the house is raised on a high basement containing a large Sub-Hall. Above are the rooms of state – intended more to impress than to be lived in – arranged in a circuit around the Marble Hall, and a saloon. Two pavilions are connected to the main block by curving corridors: one contains the family rooms, the other, the service quarters.

The pendulum was bound to swing – some turned from severe classicism to a desire for the exotic and the Picturesque combined with an interest in antiquarianism. New houses were built in the Gothick fashion while old houses such as Hardwick Hall and Charlecote Park in Warwickshire were revamped to enhance their original style. At Castle Ward in County Down and at Claydon House, Buckinghamshire, an interesting mix of classical and Gothick was achieved.

In the nineteenth century the great wealth accrued from Britain's standing as the leading trading and industrial nation saw many houses increase in size, managed by an army of staff. Symmetry was no longer a stylistic necessity, so the many new rooms that were regarded as vital components to country-house living and entertaining were often added haphazardly – the complicated layout of Cragside in Northumberland, for instance, with its towers and passages, would have been anathema to Robert Adam and Sir Nathaniel Curzon.

Of necessity, much is omitted – and plenty assumed – in this whistlestop history of the development of the country house. There are also hazards in the pages to come. First, the development of the house does not run along comfortable tracks. Halls that were once living rooms become entrance halls, and then revert to living rooms. Rooms that began as bed-sitting rooms become private sleeping chambers. Long galleries double up later as libraries. Terminology has changed too; small rooms like the closet, cabinet and wardrobe are now better known as pieces of furniture. Here the words are used in their original context. I have tried to plough a fairly straight furrow through these complexities, but there is inevitably a certain amount of cat's cradle work. Rooms, moreover, rarely stayed static. Through the centuries they filled up with furniture and furnishings, which the mind's eye must strip away to see the original form and style. In the great chamber at Lyme Park, Cheshire, for instance, the magnificent ornamentation that declares it the main room of show in the sixteenth century now appears as a backdrop to carpets, chairs and tables, vases of flowers – the comforts of later periods.

Lyme Park in Cheshire, the home of the Legh family for over five hundred years, was largely rebuilt by Sir Piers VII during the reign of Elizabeth I. The magnificent great chamber was the room where the Leghs ate and entertained away from the bustle of the great hall. The plaster overmantel of the fireplace bearing the arms of Elizabeth I, the ornate plaster ceiling and the arcaded oak wainscotting inlaid with holly and bog oak combine to emphasise the importance of the room. [AVE]

Above: The doll's house that now stands in the Steward's Hall at Uppark. In the eighteenth century these were known as baby's houses, but were for the amusement of adults rather than toys for children. This magnificent example was made *c*.1735 for the Lethieullier family, whose arms appear in the centre of the pediment, and reproduces the layout of a Georgian house. [NM]

Right: The state bedroom at Blickling Hall in Norfolk, with the bed set behind Ionic columns. While the cornice supported by the columns is decorated with ox masks – an allusion to the bull, the heraldic device of the Hobarts – the headboard of the bed displays the royal arms to emphasise the status of the family. [NM]

Antiquarianism can also confuse. The staircase hall at Blickling in Norfolk looks as if it dates from the early seventeenth century, with wooden figures of Elizabeth I and Anne Boleyn looking on. In fact, the seventeenth-century staircase was moved into the original great hall in the mid-eighteenth century, and extra figures added, including Anne and her daughter Elizabeth to remind visitors that the Boleyn family home once stood on this site. In the state bedroom at Blickling, the bed is set behind a screen created by two Ionic columns. This was the style of the seventeenth century, when the state bed, as representative of the monarch, was often set behind a balustrade so that only those of sufficient rank might approach its hallowed precincts. The Blickling bed, however, is eighteenth-century, with the ceiling or tester and headboard made up from a canopy of state that was issued to John Hobart, 2nd Earl of Buckinghamshire by George III as acknowledgement for his embassy to St Petersburg. By 1780, when this room was assembled, the idea of a bed in an inner sanctum was archaic, but Lord Buckinghamshire wanted to emphasise his prestige through this arrangement.

National Trust houses have been criticised for being set in aspic, never changing, like museums. Nothing could be further from the truth, and even some of the most recent images in this book have been overtaken by the latest research. The Trust's historic interiors are changing all the time as the staff responsible for interpreting the history of a house discover new facts.

This brief rundown on the development of the country house, of the changing functions of the rooms, and the ebb and flow of the household is of course based on the studies pioneered by Mark Girouard in *Life in the English Country House*. That book, first published in 1978, changed the way we look at our houses – they are no longer just bricks and mortar, but reflect the people who lived in them, too. I also found invaluable Gervase Jackson-Stops' *The English Country House: A Grand Tour* (1985) and the National Trust guidebooks to individual properties, which now focus on the social as well as the stylistic aspects. I am very grateful to Oliver Garnett, the Guidebook Editor, Tim Knox, Architectural Advisor to the Trust, and Adrian Tinniswood, architectural historian and expert on the sublime, for reading my text.

Above: The hall at Blickling Hall, with its Jacobean staircase. On the wall in the centre of the picture is a relief of Anne Boleyn, Henry VIII's second queen, in an arched niche. [NM]

Right: Looking towards the front door of Trerice, an Elizabethan manor house in Cornwall. The flagged screens passage separates the hall, on the right, from the kitchen quarters, to the left. [AVE]

Halls

The hall was at the heart of a substantial home in the Middle Ages. Here the owner would not only dine with his household but extend hospitality to guests and travellers. In the earliest times the lord might sleep here with his followers, but later he retreated to a solar or chamber with his family, leaving many of his servants to take their rest where they could.

Also in earlier times, verses and tales were told round the central hearth of the hall. This hearth became a more comfortable fireplace with its flue for smoke set in the wall, but the concept of entertainment in the hall continued. Often between the hall and the kitchens there ran a passage partitioned off by a screen, known as the screens passage, and above this, a gallery could be set for the use of musicians. The hall was also a place of business, where the owner held meetings, dispensed largesse and justice. An echo of this lingered at the trial of Charles I at Westminster in London – the king was adjudged in his own great hall, the principal surviving element of the medieval royal palace.

The desire for greater privacy that developed with the centuries made the need for a multi-purpose room thronged with people less important. The hall gradually became an entrance room, often grand to establish the status of the owner, populated by servants waiting for their orders and visitors awaiting admission to the more intimate parts of the house. In the nineteenth century, the wide open spaces of such a hall often succumbed to the Victorians' obsession with filling every available inch with furniture and potted plants. The hall therefore reverted to being a living room, but for a very different style of living.

The great hall at RUFFORD OLD HALL in Lancashire, built by the Hesketh family, *c.*1420. *Right*: the high table end of the hall, marked by a canopy of state to show that this was where the lord ate with his guests. To the right is a great bay window where they might withdraw for privacy. *Left*: The movable screen, intricately carved in wood, that took the place of the more usual, permanent partition. In the late sixteenth century, Sir Thomas Hesketh kept a company of players as part of his household, and reference has been found to 'willm Shakeshafte now dwellynge with me'. This adds credence to the tradition that Shakespeare lived at Rufford before returning to Stratford and marrying Anne Hathaway. He would surely have found the theatrical set piece of the remarkable screen to his liking. [AVE]

The great hall at COTEHELE in Cornwall, built in the early sixteenth century by Sir Piers Edgcumbe, looking towards the high table end, marked by the elaborate window. The hall is decorated to evoke the atmosphere of the late Middle Ages, when the walls were hung with arms and armour ready for instant use. [AVE]

The great hall at HARDWICK
NEW HALL in Derbyshire
has a quite different feel to it.
Built only seventy years later
by Elizabeth Hardwick,
Countess of Shrewsbury,
known as Bess of Hardwick,
and her architect, Robert
Smythson, it runs across the
centre of the building, rather
than along its length. Bess
adopted this idea for the
remodelling of Hardwick Old
Hall in 1585 – why she did so
is not known, but it represents
a radical departure, and gives
the desired symmetry to the
layout of the whole house.

This view is taken from
the main entrance, looking
through a screen of classical
columns – a feature that will
be seen in eighteenth-century
houses. Bess's arms, supported
by stags, are displayed on the
chimneypiece.

Bess took her meals in
her chamber, or on special
occasions in the High Great
Chamber. This hall therefore
has ceased to be used for
formal activities, but acts as
a grand entrance for visitors,
and a meeting place for servants. It was the first stage in
the procession of food from
the kitchens, which lie to the
right at the end of the hall,
up the grand staircase to the
floors above (pp. 32 and
56–7). [AVE]

Thomas Sackville, 1st Earl of Dorset, remodelled the great hall at KNOLE in Kent in the opening years of the seventeenth century. He retained the traditional layout, with a magnificent wooden screen carved by William Portington, the King's master carpenter. The whole screen may once have been painted, like the achievement of the Sackville arms in the centre of the cresting, and the Sackville leopards that guard the bottom of the doors (*above*).

On most days the family ate in private upstairs, while senior servants dined in the parlour: the hall would accommodate the household and estate servants, with the steward presiding. They sat at long tables like the one shown on the left. On formal occasions, Lord Dorset dined in state at the high table on a raised dais at the near end of the hall, out of sight in this photograph. The meal would have been accompanied by music from his private orchestra, which performed in the gallery behind the lattice windows in the upper part of the screen. [AVE]

Left: The Marble Hall at PETWORTH in West Sussex. The family home of the Percy Earls of Northumberland since the Middle Ages, Petworth was rebuilt in the 1690s following the marriage of Elizabeth, last of the line, to Charles Seymour, 6th Duke of Somerset. Seymour was known as the 'Proud Duke' and his house reflects both his awareness of the latest fashions at court and his status, which he never ceased to emphasise.

This hall provides a very grand ceremonial entrance dominated by the carvings over the fireplace, with the Seymour supporters of the bull and the unicorn flanking the Duke's arms – a reminder of his royal connection to Henry VIII's third Queen.

Entrance halls were sparsely furnished, but usually contained chairs for visitors and tradesmen. The Petworth hall chairs (*above*) are in fact older than the Marble Hall, and are very rare examples of the *sgabello* type, dating back to the time of Elizabeth Percy's grandfather, or her great grandfather, both of whom could have brought them from Italy at the beginning of the seventeenth century. Built solidly of walnut, they are not upholstered or intended for comfort. Originally they were unpainted, but are now black and gilt, and carry the Percy crescent beneath an earl's coronet. They can now be seen in the staircase hallway (p.36). [AVE]

The Hall at BENINGBROUGH in Yorkshire, completed in 1716 by the carver-architect William Thornton for John Bourchier and his wealthy heiress wife, Mary. Rising through two storeys, with giant fluted pilasters, it sounds a note of dramatic monumentality, reminiscent of Sir John Vanbrugh's work at Castle Howard, Yorkshire, where Thornton is known to have worked. During the day this room would have been the hub of the house, with servants passing through and visitors sitting on the hall chairs. At night, on occasion, it was used for large celebratory banquets. [AVE]

The Marble Hall at
KEDLESTON HALL,
Derbyshire, designed by
Robert Adam for Sir
Nathaniel Curzon in the
1760s. Recently returned
from Italy, the young architect
made good use of the classical
monuments he had seen in his
travels. This huge room, with
its twenty alabaster columns,
statues in niches, and top
lighting, suggests the open
courtyard of a Roman villa.

Adam placed the Marble
Hall and the saloon (pp.66–7)
in the centre of the main
block, with the state rooms
on one side devoted to the
Arts, and on the other to
Hospitality. The family's
private rooms and servants'
quarters were installed in
pavilions linked to the main
block by curving corridors.
This arrangement fitted with
the mid-eighteenth-century
idea of the circuit, whereby
guests could wander from
room to room at formal social
gatherings, using the Marble
Hall as their starting point.
From the outset, Kedleston
was open to the visiting
public, and we know from the
1766 diary of the Duchess of
Northumberland that the tour
took a clockwise route from
the Hall, just as it does today.
[NM]

: 24 : The Marble Hall at BERRINGTON HALL in Herefordshire, built between 1778 and 1781 by Henry Holland for the banker, Thomas Harley. The style of decoration is very severe, inspired by French neo-classicism, which Henry Holland is credited with introducing to Britain. The plaster roundels over the doors are particularly French in style, depicting trophies of arms, a reminder of more unsettled times when halls were used as armouries, as at Cotehele (p.16). [NM]

A fascination with history developed
alongside the cult of the Picturesque
and the Romantic in the late
eighteenth century. Owners who
in earlier times might have torn
down their medieval or Tudor
house as out of fashion now began
to appreciate and indeed to relish
the antiquity of their home.

When George Hammond Lucy
married Mary Elizabeth Williams in
1823, he had recently inherited
CHARLECOTE PARK, a picturesque but dilapidated mansion in
Warwickshire. The young couple
worked hard to repair Charlecote,
recalling its time of glory in the
1570s. In the great hall Sir Thomas
Lucy had entertained Elizabeth I
on one of her progresses. On
another occasion the young
William Shakespeare was said to
have been brought before him here
to answer the charge of poaching
a deer from the park, and was
punished by a flogging. He took
his revenge by caricaturing Sir
Thomas as Justice Shallow in *The
Merry Wives of Windsor*, in particular ridiculing his obsession with
his coat of arms.

George and Mary Elizabeth
Lucy enhanced the sixteenth-
century style of the great hall,
covering the walls with portraits of
their forebears, painting the ceiling
to resemble traditional wooden
beams decorated with Tudor roses,
and adding new to the old heraldic
glass in the windows. The white
luce or pike, the device that was so
important to Sir Thomas, swam
throughout the house. [AVE]

WIGHTWICK MANOR in the West Midlands also reflects the romance of the Middle Ages, though it was new built in the last years of the nineteenth century. The architect Edward Ould provided for Theodore Mander an Arts & Crafts interior based around a parlour in the style of a feudal hall (p.85). The actual entrance hall is small and reminiscent of the bays and recesses that lit the high table of a medieval great hall, with painted glass by Charles Kempe. [AVE]

Left: THE ARGORY in County Armagh, built in the 1820s for the Dublin barrister, Walter McGeough Bond, has two halls. The main entrance – the East Hall – has a classical frieze, which was still in vogue. It is filled with furniture, carpets and rugs and a long case clock: the wide open spaces seen at eighteenth-century houses are filling up with the clutter of family life. Through the doors you can see the magnificent cast iron stove in the West Hall, which also contains a sweeping cantilevered staircase. [AVE]

Right: The Central Hall at WALLINGTON in Northumberland, rising through two storeys, was created in 1853–4 from an internal courtyard. Pauline, wife of Sir Walter Trevelyan, moved in artistic and literary circles, and established Wallington as a salon for her friends, many of whom helped with the decoration of native wild flowers on the ground-floor piers of the hall. Here Lady Trevelyan would preside over the tea urn – she was a strict teetotaller – with guests such as John Ruskin and Algernon Swinburne who described the air as 'faintly laden with Pre-Raphaelite incense'. [AVE]

LANHYDROCK in Cornwall, rebuilt by Lord Robartes after a disastrous fire in 1881, has two halls, Outer and Inner. The Outer Hall was furnished as a comfortable room for living, seen here decorated for Christmas. The well-upholstered chairs are a far cry from the hall chairs of earlier centuries. The Inner Hall was more functional with its mosaic floor, serving rather as a lobby, providing access to the different parts of the house. [AVE]

The Central Hall at POLESDEN LACEY in Surrey. Polesden was bought in 1906 by the society hostess Maggie Greville, and luxuriously decorated to provide a setting for her country house parties. The room is dominated by an ornate seventeenth-century oak reredos, which had been carved by Edward Pearce (p.34) for St Matthew's Church off Cheapside in the City of London, and was bought by Mrs Greville as an imposing conversation-stopper for her hall.

In Mrs Greville's day, the Central Hall was not only intended for the reception and departure of guests, with a cloakroom and wardrobes adjoining, but it was also used as a living room where the footman would lay out drinks every evening at six o'clock. [AVE]

Staircases

Staircases depend upon going somewhere. While the great hall was the focus of the public life of a house, staircases were less important architecturally – a spiral stair in stone, brick or wood could serve in even quite a grand establishment to reach the more private living areas. But when the functions of the hall began to disperse, the main staircase took on a status of its own.

At late sixteenth-century HARDWICK HALL, Bess and her guests would make the formal procession up the stairs (*left*) from the hall (p.17), to her private chambers on the first floor, and then up again to the High Great Chamber (pp.56–7) and the state rooms beyond. The food that they consumed when they reached the top of the house would take the same route.

The Hardwick stairs are remarkable in that they meander up the house, crossing from one end to the other. Most staircases were contained within a single vertical shaft of strict form – a circle, a square or a rectangle. This formality provided splendid opportunities for the stairway and its space to be used for decoration: for fine mural painting, for plasterwork, for inlaid wood and superb ironwork.

All these are, of course, the main public staircases. The backstairs, the servants' stairs, remained modest, used by household staff to get to their own quarters and to serve the family. As Mark Girouard so memorably explained in *Life in the English Country House*, 'the gentry walking up the stairs no longer met their last night's faeces coming down them'.

By the early nineteenth century, public rooms had mostly descended to the ground floor, so staircases could again become modest, private matters, although there might always be the opportunity for a grand gesture.

Right: The staircase at Knole, remodelled by Thomas Sackville, 1st Earl of Dorset between 1605 and 1608. Guests from the great hall (pp.18–19) would climb not only to the state rooms on the first floor, but also take in the *Ascent of Man* as shown in grisaille painted decoration based on Flemish engravings. Visible in this photograph are allegories of two of the five senses, *Taste* (left) and *Hearing* (right). The snarling Sackville leopards on the newel posts would have held lanterns on staves to light the staircase. [AVE]

The great staircase at SUDBURY HALL, Derbyshire, built by George Vernon between 1660 and 1691. Vernon, who seems to have designed the house himself, was of relatively modest status, but had political ambitions. This is reflected in the superbly decorated stairs leading up to what Vernon called his 'great stairhead chamber'.

The balustrade of the stairs was carved by Edward Pearce, who had worked with Sir Christopher Wren on the rebuilding of the churches in the City of London following the fire of 1666. The baskets of flowers could be replaced by lamps at night, and possibly by baskets of real flowers for special occasions. The exuberant plasterwork was by James Pettifer and Robert Bradbury, while the murals on the underside of the stairs and on the ceiling were added later by the baroque painter, Louis Laguerre. No expense was spared to produce this dramatic set piece. [AVE]

: 36 : Louis Laguerre also worked on the very grand staircase at PETWORTH for Charles Seymour, 6th Duke of Somerset (*right*). The main theme of Laguerre's work was the story of Prometheus' punishment after stealing the secret of fire from the gods, an allusion to a severe fire at Petworth in 1714. But the Duke's pride is displayed in the *Triumph of the Duchess of Somerset*, which faces us in the photograph. Here Elizabeth Somerset is shown as Juno, being drawn in a chariot. Visitors on their way to the 'great dining room' or saloon on the first floor would feel that they were mingling in the highest company. [AVE]

This was one of Laguerre's last works, completed *c*.1720 when the grand baroque style was already going out of fashion. The great staircase at BENINGBROUGH HALL (*far right*) is also baroque in style, yet looks forward to the restrained classical style of the later eighteenth century. Marquetry panels on the half landings commemorate its completion by John and Mary Bourchier in 1716 (*see back cover*). The stairs themselves are of oak, cantilevered in three main flights, with the treads decorated in the most superb parquetry. The balusters are very thin, carved in wood to resemble wrought ironwork, and are probably the work of Huguenot craftsmen in the employ of the carver-architect, William Thornton of York. [AVE]

Left: The staircase hall at
CLAYDON HOUSE,
Buckinghamshire. Sir
Thomas Robinson, the
gentleman-architect who
advised on the design of
Claydon, wrote to his patron
Ralph, 2nd Lord Verney on
30 July 1768, 'The Staircase
will be very Noble and
Great, Mr Rose's part very
beautiful indeed, & when
compleated it will be one of
the great works of Claydon'.
And he was right. Mr Rose
was Joseph Rose, whose
graceful plasterwork of med-
allions, cameos and trophies
can be seen on the walls. The
joinery was probably the
work of the maverick genius,
Luke Lightfoot, with box,
mahogany, ebony and ivory
forming inlaid patterns on
the mahogany treads and
risers. The ironwork, by an
unknown smith, is made up
of scrolls held together by a
continuous garland of husks
and ears of corn, which rustle
as the stairs are climbed.
[AVE]

Right: The staircase hall at
BERRINGTON. Restraint
and a dependence on the
dramatic effects of space,
shadow and light were now
the order of the day. Henry
Holland planned the house
around this central staircase,
with family and guest bedrooms reached from the
landing that ran right round
the head of the stairs, lit by
a domed skylight. [NM]

After all the drama and superb craftsmanship of the Georgian staircases, the main staircase at CRAGSIDE in Northumberland (*left*) is almost an anti-climax. From 1869 the relatively modest weekend retreat from the cares of business in Newcastle was remodelled as an extensive mansion by R. Norman Shaw for the armament and engineering entrepreneur, Sir William, later Lord Armstrong. The oak staircase is ornamented with 'Queen Anne' balusters and newel posts surmounted by lions, which recall the Sackville leopards on the staircase at Knole (p.33). Again, they carry light fittings, but here they are for electricity as Cragside was the first private house in the world to be so lit. [AVE]

The Victorians were perfectly capable of making the grand gesture, however. The staircase at ARLINGTON COURT in Devon (*right*) was built in 1865 by Sir Bruce Chichester in the imperial style, rising in one splendid sweep and then dividing. Sir Bruce was a keen sailor, and this room is often compared to a yacht club. [NM]

Long Galleries

Long galleries, with their wonderful feeling of space and light, are a characteristic feature of British country houses. They apparently have two ancestors. First, the cloisters of medieval monasteries, where monks could walk and occasionally talk, study and work on their illuminated manuscripts. When William Sharington bought the former Augustinian nunnery of Lacock Abbey in Wiltshire, following the Dissolution in the 1530s, he retained the cloisters and added galleries above two of the walks.

The second ancestor was the loggia on Renaissance buildings. Edward IV built a gallery running into the garden at Eltham Palace in Kent in the 1470s, possibly inspired by the palaces of his brother-in-law, Charles the Bold, Duke of Burgundy. English galleries at this period were usually built to connect a chapel or a watergate with the main palace, taking in fine views of the garden. It was Cardinal Wolsey, always an architectural innovator, who first integrated what we would regard as the more conventional long gallery into the main structure of Hampton Court Palace. His colleague William, Lord Sandys, followed suit with two galleries – a closed one over an open arcade – at his country house, The Vyne, in Hampshire. These Tudor galleries were principally furnished with tapestries and portraits, and designed for promenading in wet weather – in his *Royal Palaces of Tudor England*, Simon Thurley describes them as 'stretch closets'.

This idea of recreational space led to galleries being used as libraries, and for hanging collections of pictures, thus becoming galleries of art.

LITTLE MORETON HALL in Cheshire was the home of the Moretons, prosperous gentlemen farmers. In the mid-fifteenth century they built a two-storeyed timber-framed house, but just over a hundred years later they added a third storey to one wing to accommodate a long gallery. This, as the *National Trust Guide* puts it, gave the house 'its curiously top-heavy appearance, like a stranded Noah's Ark, and also [pulled] the supporting timbers out of shape.'

Despite its rather rickety appearance, the Elizabethan long gallery survives. At either end of the 68-foot room are wall paintings depicting the virtues of hard work and of the power of knowledge over superstition (*left*). But the long gallery at Little Moreton Hall was not just a place for sober contemplation – a sixteenth-century tennis ball found behind the panelling shows that it was used by the family on bad weather days to play games, and for dancing and music-making. [AVE]

The magnificent gallery at HARDWICK HALL measures 162 feet in length and 26 feet in height, making it the largest surviving Elizabethan example. The dimensions were in fact dictated by the set of tapestries showing the story of Gideon, bought by Bess of Hardwick from the bankrupt estate of Sir Christopher Hatton. Over these tapestries were later hung the portraits of Bess's family, her husbands, and members of the royal family. Perhaps most important, a portrait of Elizabeth I was placed at the end of the gallery. Guests who took the processional route up the great staircase would arrive in the long gallery on the top floor of the house and be faced with this stupendous scene.

Roger North, a historian writing in the seventeenth century, explained that recesses in long galleries were for 'select companies to converse in'. The two at Hardwick were richly furnished with fine Turkey carpets on tables and embroidered cushions, and their windows probably looked out on formal knot gardens – another kind of pattern and embroidery.

Hardwick has been described as a lantern house – set high up on a hill, the great windows flash and sparkle in sunlight. At night, with candles burning in chandeliers and wall sconces, the long gallery must itself have been like a lantern, a source of wonder to those who promenaded up and down along the rush matting, listening to music from the adjoining state rooms. [AVE]

KNOLE has no fewer than four long galleries. This phenomenon may be due to the fact that Thomas Sackville, 1st Earl of Dorset, had a late medieval house with several courtyards to play with when he remodelled it in the early 1600s. He used galleries as grand approaches to sets of private apartments, so for instance, the Brown Gallery led to what became the apartment of Lady Betty Germain, while the Cartoon Gallery (*right*) gave access to the King's Bedroom and closet (pp.108–9).

The six large copies of Raphael's cartoons of the *Acts of the Apostles* hanging here lend the Cartoon Gallery its name. These were installed in the early eighteenth century, but the ornate decoration of the room dates from Thomas Sackville's time. On the left of the photograph, above the statue in a niche, can be seen two of a series of paintings of flowers arranged in vases, reflecting the idea that the

gallery should combine with the garden. Roger North wrote of the country house gallery that it should 'be easy of access, and for that reason it should be upon the first floor . . . it must be laid in the most joyous, and diverting part of the house . . . fronting the garden and viewing it from the best place'.

The Cartoon Gallery also contains part of the collection of seventeenth-century furniture that is the glory of Knole. Many pieces came to the house in the time of Charles Sackville, 6th Earl of Dorset, who was Lord Chamberlain to William III and had the pick of the furnishings of the royal palaces as his perquisite. Earlier he had served as Charles II's ambassador, travelling to France to congratulate Louis XIV on the successful completion of the secret Treaty of Dover. The gilt table and pair of candlestands shown above are thought to have been a gift from the French King. [AVE]

Long galleries provided a wonderful opportunity for the plasterer or *stuccatore* to show their skills. At CHASTLETON HOUSE in Oxfordshire, built between 1607 and 1612 by a wealthy lawyer, Walter Jones, the long gallery has a spectacular barrel vaulted ceiling (*above*). The plasterwork is decorated with strapwork intertwining around roses, daisies and fleurs de lys, enlivened by grotesque painted masks in the spandrels at one end. As at Little Moreton Hall, balls and shuttlecocks have been found under the floorboards, and even as late as 1852 the owner recorded in his diary 'it rained so much we betook ourselves to the long room for exercise.' [NM]

The long gallery at BLICKLING HALL in Norfolk (*right*) is almost exactly contemporary with Chastleton. It too boasts a fine plaster ceiling, created in five months in 1620 by the plasterer Edward Stanyon for the sum of £95 19s. The ceiling is divided into a series of panels by embossed ribs marked with pendants. The eleven central panels show heraldic achievements, the five senses, and Learning.

At the time the long gallery was used by the Hobart family as a place of recreation and for displaying family portraits. But a century later Learning became particularly apt when John Hobart, 1st Earl of Buckinghamshire, inherited an important book collection from a distant relative, Richard Ellys. The portraits came down and bookshelves were erected in their stead, though the shelves shown in this photograph date from the nineteenth century. This change in use from conventional gallery to a library was one that quite frequently took place – in the eighteenth century Robert Adam, for instance, made a similar conversion at Syon House in Middlesex, and in the nineteenth century books were installed in the long gallery at Sudbury. [NM]

The long gallery at SUDBURY HALL, just over 138 feet in length and completed for George Vernon c.1676. It is most unusual to find a long gallery in a house of this period, but given Vernon's pride and ambition, he may well have conceived the gallery as a way of stressing the antiquity of his family. Whatever his motives, this is a magnificent room decorated in the fashionable style of the time. The ceiling, by the plasterers Bradbury and Pettifer, is full of fun, from the heads of emperors which may caricature contemporary notables such as Charles II and his brother James, Duke of York, to grasshoppers dancing round the central rosette. [AVE]

In the eighteenth century picture galleries – as opposed to galleries with pictures – became a feature of British country houses. At WIMPOLE HALL in Cambridgeshire the architect Henry Flitcroft, undertaking a series of alterations in 1742, opened up three cabinets (small rooms) into one long room on the ground floor. This was to be Lord Hardwicke's new picture gallery, where he could hang the best of his collection of Old Master paintings, and an Italian *stuccatore*, Giuseppe Artari, provided the decorative plasterwork of the wall panels. Columns mark the position of the former dividing walls. [AVE]

The Wyndhams of PETWORTH, like their ancestors, the Percys and the Seymours (p.21), were great patrons of the arts. Charles Wyndham, 2nd Earl of Egremont, built up a fine collection of antique sculpture, mostly acquired from Italy despite the Papacy's stringent control on the export of classical remains. These were housed in a long rectangular gallery at Petworth, specially designed by the architect Matthew Brettingham in 1754 by enclosing an open arcade.

Lord Egremont died suddenly in 1763 as a result of a turtle dinner too far, and his art collection and houses were inherited by his son George, the 3rd Earl. His collecting taste was rather different. He commissioned landscapes and paintings with historical and literary themes from contemporary British artists. On occasion he even welcomed the artist and their family into his home at Petworth: the painter J.M.W.Turner, for instance, spent several years working in a studio above the chapel.

To accommodate his collection alongside that of his father, he first added a parallel corridor, and later a square bay. *Above*: Some of the 2nd Earl's antique statuary. *Right*: The Central Corridor with contemporary paintings and sculpture commissioned by the 3rd Earl. [AVE]

Far left: The gallery at CRAGSIDE was originally built in 1872–4 as a museum to house Sir William Armstrong's scientific, geological and natural history specimens. In 1879, however, it was turned into a gallery to display the best of his picture collection, lit by twenty of Joseph Swan's incandescent light bulbs. As in long galleries from earlier centuries, it was hung with portraits of Sir William, his family and friends. In addition, though, were two pictures by Henry Hetherington Emmerson that reflected his very Victorian preoccupation with death, the forces of nature and the faithfulness of animals to their masters: *Orphan of the Storm* and *Faithful unto Death*. This photograph was taken in 1994, before the pictures were returned to their original, more crowded arrangement. [AVE]

When Mrs Greville decided to create her version of a long gallery at POLESDEN LACEY (*left*) in 1906, she copied the plaster ceiling of the barrel vault at Jacobean Chastleton (p.48), albeit on a smaller scale. Her Picture Corridor, where many of her paintings, fine furniture and china were displayed, ran round three sides of the central courtyard. [AVE]

Living Rooms

In medieval times the principal living room of a house was the hall, and for privacy the family usually retired to a solar, which doubled up as a sleeping chamber. The desire for more privacy, combined with a desire for greater comfort meant that in sixteenth-century establishments such as Hardwick Hall separate bedchambers were provided for the family. Eating and entertaining took place in the great chamber or the parlour, often with a withdrawing room attached – a room that was a retreat from the main public area. In time the great chamber was renamed the saloon, and the withdrawing room became simply the drawing room.

Grander establishments often also contained state apartments, set aside for the entertainment of royal visitors and honoured guests. At Hardwick, for instance, Bess had her chamber and withdrawing room on the first floor, but on special occasions she entertained in the state apartments, including the long gallery (pp.44–5), the High Great Chamber, and withdrawing chamber on the second floor.

A much later set of state apartments was built by Robert Adam at Kedleston Hall in Derbyshire in the 1760s. These rather quaintly included a state bedroom, dressing room and wardrobe – a room where clothes were stored, rather than a piece of furniture. By the end of the eighteenth century, however, the concept of state rooms had become outmoded in all but the grandest houses. By this time too it had become the norm to set aside a room – or indeed rooms – specifically for eating (see pp.88 & ff.), so that living rooms were for recreation and entertainment. Their number and their particular use proliferated, reaching an apogee in later Victorian houses with parts of the house given over to masculine activities like billiards and smoking, another part to female occupations in the boudoir and the drawing room, with the dining room as a sort of neutral ground.

Left: The High Great Chamber at HARDWICK, one of the state apartments on the top floor, reached by the great staircase (p.32). Bess of Hardwick always hoped that Elizabeth I might visit, and the High Great Chamber is furnished with allusions to the Queen. While Bess's arms are on the fireplace in the great hall (p.17), the chimneypiece here carries the royal coat of arms. The superb painted plaster frieze above the tapestries depicts the court of Diana the virgin goddess and huntress, a compliment to Elizabeth, the Virgin Queen. Diana herself appears directly over the chairs of state under a canopy, which is where Bess would have received her visitors and entertained them to dinner or supper on tables brought in for the occasion. [AVE]

He would have eaten here, leaving

When KNOLE was first built in the fifteenth century as a country house for the Archbishops of Canterbury this huge room, now known as the ballroom, was the solar. The word derives from the Latin *sol*, the sun, as these rooms were usually located on an upper floor and were intended to catch the sunshine. The solar at Knole was the Archbishop's chief living room where he retired after eating in the great hall. It continued this role in the early seventeenth century, as Thomas Sackville's great chamber, standing at the head of the main staircase. He would have eaten here, leaving his steward to superintend the household dining in the great hall.

As befits the status of such a room, the decoration is very rich, produced by the King's craftsmen. The elaborate plaster frieze with its mermaids and grotesque figures, and the ceiling decorations of fruit and foliage were the work of Richard Dungan. The ornate oak panelling was by William Portington, while the delicious chimney-piece and overmantel (*see detail*) were made by Cornelius Cure for the grand total of £26 10s. [AVE]

The Tudor great chamber at TRERICE in Cornwall (*left*), like that at Knole, developed from an earlier, medieval solar. The Arundells of Trerice were not as grand as the Sackvilles of Knole, but they have produced a richly decorated room to reflect its status, making bold use of the plasterwork on the barrel ceiling and over the fireplace. [AVE]

HAM HOUSE in Surrey was furnished in the 1670s in the most fashionable style by John Maitland, Duke of Lauderdale, and his Duchess, Elizabeth. Their grand reception rooms were on the first floor, with a great dining room leading off the staircase. This room has since been turned into a gallery for the hall below, but the room to which the guests withdrew, the North Drawing Room, survives in all its splendour (*right*). Perhaps most impressive of all is the marble chimneypiece with its surround of carved and gilt twisted columns, derived from Raphael's cartoons of the *Acts of the Apostles* (see p.46), that gives the room an exotic Continental flavour. [AVE]

By the late seventeenth century the principal living room was often known as the parlour. This harks back to medieval monastic establishments, where the rule of silence prevailed except in one room where the monks or nuns could relax and *parler* – talk to each other. Later generations preferred the more sophisticated 'saloon' from the French, *salon*. George Vernon's parlour of the 1670s at SUDBURY, now called the saloon, is set at the bottom of his very lavish staircase (pp.34–5), and continues the rich decorative scheme provided by the plasterwork of Bradbury and Pettifer, and the carved woodwork of Edward Pearce. [AVE]

The saloon at BENINGBROUGH HALL dates from the early years of the eighteenth century. It is a room of considerable size, running along five bays on the garden side of the house, and would have been used for large gatherings, for county balls, and routs to celebrate important family occasions. The decoration is less exuberant than at Sudbury, and strongly architectural, with giant fluted Corinthian pilasters to enhance the sense of grandeur. [AVE]

These rooms would have been sparsely, though richly furnished with textiles. When the family wished to dine, gate-legged tables would have been carried in and set up, and chairs and stools – ranged along the wall when not in use – brought into the centre of the room.

In 1746 Matthew Fetherstonhaugh inherited a fortune from a distant cousin on condition that he acquired a baronetcy and an estate. He complied with both attractive obligations, purchasing the late seventeenth-century house at UPPARK, perched on the top of the Sussex Downs. Sir Matthew remodelled his house, moving away from the formal style of the early eighteenth century and adopting a more relaxed style of living. The former entrance hall, a high room, was recreated as the saloon, with a stunningly beautiful plaster ceiling (*right*). The paintings were brought back from a Grand Tour of Italy with his wife Sarah Lethieullier. [NM]

Above: The Little Parlour at Uppark. Formerly, the entrance hall was flanked by two parlours, intimate rooms where the family might relax, talk and eat. The Great Parlour (now the Red Drawing Room) was probably the main eating room, although the Little Parlour is recorded in the 1705 inventory as containing four tables, which suggests that it was probably used for less formal meals. The furniture seen here dates from the 1770s. [NM]

When Robert Adam was called in to KEDLESTON by Sir Nathaniel Curzon in 1760, three previous architects had already left their mark on the layout – a central block with pavilions. The central area was to be the public part of the house, the pavilions for family life and for the servants' quarters. In the centre of the main block lay the Marble Hall (p.23), with a circular saloon behind.

The saloon, like the other rooms of parade at Kedleston, is splendidly monumental. Based on the Pantheon in Rome, one of the most admired buildings of classical antiquity, its coffered dome rises to 62 feet. Everything in the room is curved, from the paintings set into the walls, to the doorcases, chairs and settees. This great space was intended for parties, so to reduce the Derbyshire chill, a carpet was made to reflect the decoration of the ceiling. In addition, cast iron stoves were built to Robert Adam's designs: servants would stoke them from passages behind the saloon so as not to disturb guests' conversations. [NM]

In 1768 John Parker, 1st Lord Boringdon commissioned Robert Adam to create a suite of rooms along the east front of his country house at SALTRAM just outside Plymouth in Devon. In his inimitable manner, Adam designed almost every detail to produce a series of dramatic rooms in the fashionable neo-classical style.

The Velvet Drawing Room (*left*) took its name from the red silk velvet hangings that have now been replaced by red flock. The screen of Corinthian columns picked out in gilt provides a fitting prelude to the magnificent saloon beyond (*right*). The great coved ceiling contains paintings by Antonio Zucchi, including Diana hunting, in acknowledgement of Lord Boringdon's love for the chase. The Axminster carpet echoes the patterns of the ceiling, but in clear blues, pinks and greys, with touches of red and black.

The saloon was conceived by Robert Adam for parties, and one held in 1810 was recorded by Frances Parker, Countess of Morley: 'The Saloon was prepared for the dancing and looked quite brilliant and beautiful – we lighted it by hanging lamps over the windows and putting a quantity of candles over the doors, the places in which they were fixed being concealed by large wreaths and festoons of leaves and flowers beautiful to behold. The floor was chalked after an exquisite design of my own, by a celebrated artist from Plymouth ... round the room we had two rows of seats affording comfortable anchorage for about 200 persons.' [AVE]

By the end of the eighteenth century, the formal idea of sets of private apartments had been overtaken by a more informal way of living. Nevertheless some seclusion from the main public rooms of a house was still desired. For ladies, this usually took the form of a boudoir, from the French *bouder*, to be sulky.

At BERRINGTON HALL, the boudoir is located next door to the drawing room, with double doors to protect the privacy of the women of the Harley family. Servants could bring refreshments from the kitchen below via a door in the alcove, while a cupboard behind the shutters was designed to hold two chamber-pots. The room was designed by Henry Holland in the late 1770s in the neo-classical style, with a curved alcove running the length of the boudoir, screened off from the rest of the room by Ionic columns of blue scagliola. [AVE]

The boudoir at CASTLE WARD in County Down presents a very different picture. In the 1760s when Bernard Ward and his wife Anne planned their house, they could not agree on its style, so agreed to disagree, with Bernard adopting the classical style (*see frontispiece*), and Anne going for Gothick. Naturally, being her domain, the boudoir reflected her taste, and is dominated by the voluptuous curves of the plaster ceiling based on the fan vaulting of Henry VII's Chapel in Westminster Abbey. Sir John Betjeman said that being in this room was like standing under the udders of a cow. [AVE]

: 72 : The saloon at CASTLE WARD is also Gothick, with traceried windows, ogival mirrors and even battlements on the carved wooden overmantel. In the midst of all this Gothicism hangs a picture of Bernard Ward defiantly holding a drawing of his – Palladian – side of the house. The divergence of views on architectural style developed into a more serious rift in their marriage, with Lady Anne moving out and settling in Bath soon after the house was finished. [AVE]

The Yellow Drawing Room at WIMPOLE HALL (*left*) is a very dramatic room. Just as Henry Flitcroft had designed a gallery for the 1st Lord Hardwicke's Old Masters in the 1740s (p.51), so John Soane created this T-shaped room in 1793 to house the gems from the picture collection of the 3rd Earl. But it was also to double up as a grand reception room for county balls and concerts, so the ingenious Soane took up three old rooms on the ground floor and four on the first, producing a huge space almost like a church, with the chimneypiece as the altar and the top-lit dome as the crossing with semi-circular apses on either side. [AVE]

An equally dramatic space was created at ARLINGTON COURT when in the 1860s Sir Bruce Chichester threw three rooms into one to produce a tripartite gallery 70 feet long, punctuated by Ionic columns (*right*). When only a small space was required, folding screens were brought in.

In the foreground is the morning room, taking advantage of the sun on the east side of the house. Its decoration dates from the 1830s, and was probably supplied by John Gregory Crace. Beyond lies an ante-room, designed by Thomas Lee, who had trained in the office of Sir John Soane, and it very much reflects his style. Beyond again lies the White Drawing Room. [NM]

The drawing room at CHARLECOTE (*above*) is decorated in the Elizabethan Revival style that George and Mary Elizabeth Lucy deemed appropriate for their ancient house. Decorated in the 1850s, it combines Victorian comfort with antiquarian touches, such as the strapwork on the plaster ceiling and a seventeenth-century East Indian settee in ebony, which the Lucys believed was made for the Elizabethan court.

Equally exotic is the morning room at KNIGHTSHAYES COURT in Devon (*right*). Sir John Heathcoat-Amory, having inherited the largest lace-making enterprise in the world, began to build a house fitting for his status in 1869. His first architect was William Burges, whose fervent imagination proved too much for his patron, and the decoration of the house was completed by John Diblee Crace.

Burges designed the morning room as an octagon, which he wanted to fill in the richest way possible, with 'Turkish, Persian, Indian and other Eastern production' carpets, and walls panelled in ebonised wood framing tiles painted with flowers and birds. Above this he planned a painted frieze of 'Heroes and Heroines of the Fairytales'. But Heathcoat-Amory suppressed much of this extraordinary scheme, retaining only the principal architectural elements such as the doors carved with family monograms. The compartmental ceiling designed by Crace was hidden by a plain white ceiling until restoration work took place in 1995. It features the motto 'Health Long Life Wealth Happiness'. [AVE]

The idea of having apartments for men and for women goes back many centuries – Tudor palaces had the King's side and the Queen's side – and Ham House shows this compartment-alisation well, having the Duke's apartments, the Duchess's, and the state apartments (pp.110–112). This division survived into Victorian times with the idea that there should be masculine rooms and feminine rooms. In *The Gentleman's House* published in 1864 Robert Kerr wrote that the dining room was masculine, and the drawing room feminine, their characteristics being 'masculine importance' and 'feminine delicacy'.

KNIGHTSHAYES, like every fashionable Victorian country house, had its masculine domains – the smoking room and the billiard room – in this case located at opposite sides of the house. The billiard room is equipped with its own lavatory and washroom so that play could continue well into the night. Around the ceiling William Burges set carved animal corbels representing the Seven Deadly Sins plus an eighth depicting an owl, Symbol of Wisdom. Despite the masculine style of most billiard rooms, it was a game often played by ladies. [AVE]

The drawing room at Knightshayes was designed by Burges to reflect the fact that it is 'the lady's apartment essentially', so he chose a chivalric theme, with the chimneypiece featuring *The Assault on the Castle of Love*. A columned gallery was designed to run behind the mantelpiece so that Victorian ladies might join their painted counterparts in the Castle and wave at the gentlemen below.

Sir John Heathcoat-Amory again halted the work and the room is now decorated in the rich but more subdued style of Crace, though Burges' ceiling has recently been revealed, with its extraordinary golden concavities that resemble jelly moulds.

The room is now comparatively sparsely furnished, but an inventory taken in 1899 lists no less than six settees, seventeen tables, twelve armchairs and ten chairs among its contents. Leading out of the drawing room is a conservatory. Although this dates from the 1960s, it was very much the fashion of the Victorian period, regarded as a living room in its own right, for sitting out during parties, or simply for the family to relax amongst ferns and palms. [AVE]

Nineteenth-century country houses positively exploded with rooms. Houses new built, like the Duke of Westminster's Eaton Hall in Cheshire, were enormous in scale, while existing buildings were extended to provide them with the multiplicity of rooms for living and for entertaining that wealthy Victorians considered necessary.

CRAGSIDE, the country house of Sir William Armstrong, started off as a comparatively modest affair, a weekend retreat from his business life in Newcastle upon Tyne. But in 1869 Armstrong called in the architect R. Norman Shaw to transform the house into a proper country mansion, and over the next fifteen years the various additions created its very complex layout. The drawing room is Armstong's last and grandest addition, begun in 1883 and ready for the visit of the Prince and Princess of Wales the following year. Guests would gather here before taking the rather tortuous route to the dining room, and ladies would return for tea and coffee, leaving their menfolk at table.

The room is dominated by a great chimneypiece designed by Norman Shaw's chief assistant, W. R. Lethaby. It is Italian Renaissance in style but also contains an inglenook so that Sir William might sit cosily by his fire, where only turf was burned in the grate. [AVE]

The Victorian distinction between the masculine and feminine parts of a house can be seen very clearly at LANHYDROCK, which was rebuilt in 1881. Lord Robartes instructed his architect, Richard Coad, to provide him with a 'modest and unpretentious family home'. It would now seem far from modest, but such was the standard of the time. Not only were the main family rooms divided into male and female areas, but there was a suite of rooms set aside as nursery accommodation for the Robartes children, and strict segregation divided the servants from the family, and male from female.

Right: Lady Robartes' Boudoir is light and feminine, furnished with comfortable chairs and filled with drawings and paintings of her children. [AVE]

Above: The smoking room provides the male equivalent, a warm mellow room with deep-buttoned armchairs, pictures and mementoes of school and university along with trophies of the field and the stream. [AVE]

The great parlour at WIGHTWICK MANOR was added in 1893 and planned as the principal room of the house. It was intended to give the impression of a medieval great hall with all the comforts of a late Victorian living room. A screens passage runs across the end, with a minstrel's gallery – in fact, a bedroom landing – over the top. The inglenook fireplace carries a motto in medieval French that translates as 'A welcoming house puts its faith in God.' But the Mander family did not have to rely on the fire alone, radiators are carefully concealed behind grilles in the panelling. The room was used as an informal living room for relaxing, listening to music and for parties.

The furnishings and fittings reflect the artistic taste of the 1890s, with woollen panels woven by William Morris below the painted frieze by Charles Kempe – an interesting echo of the style of the High Great Chamber at Hardwick (pp.56–7). [AVE]

Mrs Greville's architect for
POLESDEN LACEY, Arthur
Davis, was asked to design a
saloon 'fit to entertain
Maharajahs in'. He duly provided a glittering room using
carvings and panels from a
salone of an Italian *palazzo*,
*c.*1700, complete with painted
canvases let into the ceiling
and masses of mirror glass to
increase the glitter. A portrait
of Mrs Greville presides over
the room, where every surface
was filled with pictures, lamps
and vases of flowers, in the
style fashionable at the beginning of the twentieth century.
Beverley Nichols, a frequent
visitor to Polesden Lacey,
found it 'really quite appalling
. . . over-gilt, over-velveted,
over-mirrored like an
extremely expensive bordel'.

Left: One of the chimney-
pieces with a Louis XV
clock, flanked by Chinese
eighteenth-century cranes
and bronze and ormolu
Louis XVI candelabra.
[AVE]

Eating Rooms

The medieval eating room of castles and country houses was the great hall. The master and his family were seated at the upper end, often on a raised dais, while the rest of the household ate at long trestle tables running down the hall. Their food was often organised into messes – servings for a set number of people. This communal eating, like other aspects of daily life, declined as the family sought more privacy in a great chamber or a parlour. An interesting interim arrangement can be seen at LITTLE MORETON HALL (*left*), where a round table was installed in the bay window of the great hall in 1559.

References to eating or dining rooms begin to appear in late seventeenth-century inventories and records, but even then the room would not be set up permanently for meals: the tables, which were usually gate-legged with folding tops, were kept against the walls or in corridors, to be brought in when needed. Chairs would also be set against the wall and brought to the middle of the room.

The dining style that prevailed right up to Victorian times is now described as *à la française*. Like meals served in Chinese restaurants today, the various dishes of a course would all be brought to the table together and laid out so that guests might have a chance to sample the different foods on offer. There were usually two main courses, with meat and fish dishes served at the same time as what we would call sweets and puddings. A third course of sweetmeats, fruit and nuts might be provided on special occasions, often in another room. This course was called the banquet, or later the dessert.

In the nineteenth century, the dining style *à la russe* was introduced, where different courses were brought to the table, as now in restaurants and at formal dinner parties. The dining table, with chairs arranged round it, had become a permanent feature in the dining room. The dessert survived as the final course, and the long mahogany tables looked particularly well for this part of the meal.

Right: The dining room at BADDESLEY CLINTON in Warwickshire. It was furnished with oak panelling and armorial glass by Henry Ferrers, who lived there in the late sixteenth century and was known as 'the Antiquary' because of his interest in his family history. Although the style of table setting is Victorian, the table is of the gate-leg type, which could be folded up and stored when not in use. The oak court cupboard, dating from the reign of Charles I, was an early form of sideboard where plate could be displayed. [AVE]

The state dining room at KEDLESTON was designed by Robert Adam in the 1760s as part of the circuit of rooms devoted to Hospitality. In his writings Adam recommends that dining rooms 'instead of being hung with damask, tapestry, etc., they are always finished with stucco, and adorned with statues and paintings, that they may not retain the smell of victuals.' At Kedleston he fixed upon paintings, which are set into the walls so that the scheme today is as he planned it. On the lower tier are pastoral scenes, reminiscent of the landscape park outside the windows, but above are pictures of dead animals, a curious but typical digestive aid for eighteenth-century diners.

Perhaps the most striking feature of this room is the recessed alcove, where Adam designed a buffet that reproduced the medieval idea of displaying plate. Here, however, he produced a superb neo-classical version, with salvers, knife boxes, vases and a perfume burner, set on the curving tables. Below stood wine coolers and cisterns. In the style *à la française* glasses were not placed on the table, but would be brought to the diners by the footmen on duty at the buffet. The glasses were rinsed after use, and the wine kept cool in the huge containers.

Every detail of decoration was attended to by Robert Adam. He wanted this room to be like a Roman dining room, with allusions to Bacchus, the god of wine, in the plasterwork ceiling and on the fireplace. In front of the fire was placed the handsome plate warmer designed by 'Athenian' Stuart in the style of a huge classical vase (*right*). [NM]

The dining room at SALTRAM (*left*) was originally designed by Robert Adam as a library, but altered ten years later in 1780 when Lord Boringdon decided to bring it within range of his new kitchen. The paintings on the ceiling and over the doors therefore allude to library-oriented classical subjects rather than to the art of dining. On the right can be seen the curved tables of the buffet, with one of a pair of green vases designed by Adam for use as wine-coolers.

In medieval and Tudor times, dinner, the main meal of the day, was usually served at midday, while breakfast was taken in one's chamber – if one had a bedroom – and supper might be provided before bedtime. Dinner-time gradually became later and later through the centuries, so that the Parkers of Saltram in the 1780s would have dined at around 4 p.m., having consumed a nuncheon or luncheon, a midday snack. Breakfast had now become quite an elaborate and hearty meal, taken in the morning or breakfast room between 9 and 11 a.m.

The morning room at Saltram (*right*) is filled with paintings, including several portraits of the Parker family by Sir Joshua Reynolds, a family friend. It was used both for breakfast and for more informal dinners. In 1811 Lady Boringdon's brother, the Rev. Thomas Talbot, was not very complimentary about a morning room dinner: 'His Lrdship and Lyship seated opp. each other in the middle of the Table in the french taste: – in the Centre of the Table, *Nothing* – the first Course some white Soup opp. Lrd. B – some Soles opp. Ly B. and nothing else – the 2nd [course] had small made dishes lengthwise of the table and nothing else – the 3rd [course] some Game and 3 or 4 small Dishes of sweet or savoury at Random – then the Dessert … with some undrinkable Port, bad Madeira, Sherry and mediocre Claret planted at the 4 Corners – on a Side Table some Roast Mutton and boil'd Beef completed the Repast.' [AVE]

The dining room at UPPARK, which was designed by Humphry Repton in 1812–13 for Sir Harry Fetherstonhaugh. Sir Harry, who inherited Uppark in 1774, deeply worried his mother by his penchant for liaisons with working girls: in 1780 he plucked Emma Hart from an establishment called the Temple of Health and installed her at Uppark, where she is said to have entertained his friends by dancing naked on the dining-room table. Emma went on to become Lady Hamilton and mistress of Admiral Nelson. The table survived Repton's alterations and can be seen with chairs dating from the 1760s.

Beyond the dining room is the servery, where food brought along underground passages from the kitchens was given the finishing touch by Monsieur Moget, Sir Harry's French chef. The magnificent stained glass window shows banqueting scenes from the sixteenth century in the roundel, and from classical Greece in the strip below the rose; this was inspired by the Elgin Marbles which had recently arrived in England from Athens. Repton intended the window to be seen by day and by night; the effect of the latter 'will be magic as all the light may proceed from this window from Argand [oil] lamps properly adjusted from behind.' [AVE]

Right: The dining room at CHARLECOTE decorated, like the rest of the house, in the Elizabethan Revival style of the 1830s. The Lucys had called in Thomas Willement, antiquarian and Heraldic Artist to George IV, to mastermind the interior decoration. But it is very different from Tudor eating rooms. The table was permanently set up in the middle of the room with chairs arranged around it. Each course would be brought from the kitchen through a door behind the screen and served to guests by footmen under the supervision of the butler in the style *à la russe*. The table is shown here laid for the dessert course, with ornate table silver and flower arrangements running down the centre.

In 1858 Mary Elizabeth Lucy bought the colossal Charlecote buffet (*above*) for an equally colossal sum, £1,600. Carved by J.M.Willcox and his Warwick school of carvers, it represents the resources of nature and trophies of the chase. Like Adam's buffet in the recess of the dining room at Kedleston (p.90), it recalls the medieval practice of displaying plate in the great hall or great chamber. [AVE]

Right: The dining room at KNIGHTSHAYES decorated by J.D.Crace. The ceiling carries quotations from Robert Burns, such as 'Keep thy tongue and keep thy friends'.

Dining rooms of the later nineteenth century often had a main table set in the centre of the room for lunch, dinner and formal suppers, while a second table was installed in a bay window for breakfast. Victorian breakfasts were hearty affairs with a variety of hot dishes such as scrambled eggs and devilled kidneys laid out on plate warmers on the sideboard. One visitor to Knightshayes in the early years of the twentieth century recalls 'On a hunting day it was such fun . . . the sideboard loaded with cold ham, galantine and other meats, sliced bread and a pile of greaseproof paper and you just went and made your own sandwiches and took as much as ever you wanted.' [AVE]

Left: The dining room at WIGHTWICK MANOR, decorated with William Morris & Co. paper and curtains, and a fine hand-knotted carpet. The room faces east, to provide sunlight for breakfast, which would have been taken in the window recess, but keeping the room cool for the later meals of the day. Dishes were carried to the serving room and china pantry behind a hatch in the corner of the room, where hotplates and heated serving dishes kept the food warm until the appropriate moment when it would appear from behind a screen.

By this time formal dinner was usually served as late as 9 p.m. Guests would assemble in the drawing room and then process to the dining room. At the end of the meal, which often consisted of several courses, the ladies would return to the drawing room, leaving the men at the table to ruminate on politics and triumphs sporting and sexual. In the case of Theodore Mander at Wightwick, a Wolverhampton councillor and chairman of the school board, the politics were Liberal. [AVE]

Left: The dining room at POLESDEN LACEY. Most of Mrs Greville's furniture for this room has been sold, but it is known that in the early years of the twentieth century she had a traditional English dining table, covered always with a linen tablecloth, as shown here. In 1934 a lacquer circular table was installed, a style that came from America. For dinners the table was laden with old silver, and such was the profusion that there was no room for flower arrangements.

Mrs Greville was one of the leading society hostesses of the early twentieth century, providing delicious food at country-house weekends. Her guests were also entertained by the contrast between her two butlers – Bole, who looked and behaved like a butler,

and Bacon, who claimed to be a communist and enjoyed his drink. On one famous occasion, Mrs Greville noticed the butler was swaying ominously, so sent a note via a footman with a salver to tell him to leave the room. The butler read the note, put it back on the salver and presented it to the distinguished politician, Sir Austen Chamberlain.

Large parties were held in the saloon (p.87), while more intimate gatherings were held in the Tea Room (*above*). Beverley Nichols recalled, 'Maggie's teas were terrific, with great Georgian teapots and Indian or China, and muffins and cream cakes and silver kettles sending up their steam, and Queen Mary saying "Indian, if you please, and no sugar"...' [AVE]

Bedrooms

The bedchamber in medieval homes was the solar, where the lord or master could retire to sleep. It doubled up as his place for private living, and was in effect a bed-sitting room, where he could conduct business, take his breakfast and be with his family and body servants. At night a servant might sleep in the chamber on straw pallets or in a truckle, a bed on wheels that was stored under the main bed during the day.

By the sixteenth century, the number of bedrooms had begun to multiply, so that Bess of Hardwick's family each had their own chamber, and so did her upper servants, accommodated in the Old Hall which stood hard by her new house at Hardwick. The bed would consist of a bedstead, a wooden structure, and its furnishings – hangings, mattress, linen and pillows. For the wealthy the furnishing could be very ornate, making the bed the most expensive item in the house. In the greatest houses there would be a bed of estate or state bed. This would be ready for the arrival of the monarch or a very distinguished guest, but was also an important element in the public display of the owner. At Hardwick, for instance, Bess set up a magnificent bed as part of her sequence of state rooms on the upper floor. Decorated with a valance of black velvet embossed with cloth of gold and silver, embroidered with gold and pearl, and with curtains of yellow and white damask, it had been made for her second marriage.

The idea of the private apartment developed in the later seventeenth century, with the bedchamber accompanied by closets. Often situated on the ground floor at the corner of the building, they represented the most intimate rooms at the end of an enfilade or series of chambers. An elaborate ritual could be observed as to who might enter which rooms within this series. This very formal way of living gradually dispersed in the eighteenth and nineteenth centuries, with the closet becoming a dressing room, and bedrooms ascending to the upper floors of the house, where greater privacy might be enjoyed.

The Blue Bedroom at HARDWICK HALL. The bed was made in 1629 for Christian Bruce, widow of the 2nd Earl of Devonshire, its original hangings remounted on blue damask. At the end of the bed is a coffer where clothes and linen would be kept – the hanging wardrobe was an early nineteenth-century innovation. The room is hung with tapestries showing gods and planets, bought by Bess of Hardwick in 1591/2. [NM]

Bedsteads were often very plain, wooden structures, which could be hidden under elaborate hangings. But both these beds at COTEHELE have elaborately carved posts and headboards. *Right*: In Queen Anne's Room is a Tudor bed with gilt and painted posts. The curtains are of early eighteenth-century woollen damask, the valances around the top are of late seventeenth-century silk. *Above*: The bed in King Charles's Room is a complex affair apparently made from the bulbous posts of an Elizabethan table (*see back cover*) and a headboard that could have been the overmantel of a fireplace. The hangings are of crewelwork applied to woollen backing. On the cabinet next to the bed is a mirror of polished metal, dating from about 1625. Looking glasses began to appear some twenty or thirty years later, and Samuel Pepys makes reference in his diary of the 1660s to 'counterfeit windows' of reflecting glass which were so useful for bedchambers and their closets. [AVE]

KNOLE has a fine collection of seventeenth-century beds and accompanying furniture because in his capacity as Lord Chamberlain, Charles Sackville, 6th Earl of Dorset had the pick of the furnishings from the royal palaces. The Spangle Bed, however, was acquired in the 1620s by his grandfather, Lionel Cranfield, when he was Master of the Great Wardrobe to James I. It has been much altered to give it the height that characterised late seventeenth- and early eighteenth-century beds, but the hangings are original, of crimson and white silk sewn with thousands of tiny sequins that shimmered in the candlelight.

The matching suite of furniture includes an x-framed chair of state and high stools. Many great land-owners were constantly on the move from house to house, taking their furniture with them. The bedstead would normally stay put, but its hangings and linen would be transported by wagon. The x-chairs were constructed so that they too could be folded up and taken on their travels. They were often placed at the end of the bed so that the lord or lady might receive honoured guests seated in the chair. [AVE]

The King's Bedroom at KNOLE, with its magnificent state bed, probably made for James, Duke of York for his marriage to Mary of Modena in 1673. The hangings are of cloth of gold backed by cherry coloured satin, with crimson and white ostrich feathers cutting a dash on the tops of the bedposts. The accompanying bed furniture includes chairs and stools carved with little cupids holding bows and quivers, together with billing doves – all very appropriate for a marriage bed.

The King's Bedroom also contains silver furniture dating from the 1660s and 70s. In the left foreground is a toilet set, consisting of a mirror, bowls and scent jars, hairbrushes and even an eye-bath. The word toilet derives from the silk cover or 'toylett' which was set up on a dressing table – and most wealthy ladies and gentlemen would have such a set in their bedchamber, though this is the earliest of silver to survive. Flanking the bed are two small mirrors with sconces to reflect the candlelight. [AVE]

Along the corridor from the King's Bedroom is the closet or dressing room, with its late seventeenth-century hangings of green mohair. In the right foreground can be seen the red velvet top of a close stool, which held a chamber-pot. This was yet another piece of furniture acquired by Charles Sackville, Earl of Dorset from Whitehall Palace, and would have originally stood in a 'dark closet' across the passage. [AVE]

HAM HOUSE in Surrey was furnished in the 1670s in the very latest fashion by John Maitland, Duke of Lauderdale, and his Duchess, Elizabeth. Their private apartments, each consisting of a bedchamber, a dressing room and a closet, are on the ground floor on either side of the Marble Dining Room. At some stage the Duke swapped his bedroom with the Duchess, making it rather difficult to follow the sequence of the rooms today. But it is possible to evoke the lifestyle of leading members of the Stuart court by looking at their respective closets.

The Duke's Closet (*far right*) was completed in 1674, including 'panes to double ye sashes' – double glazing – to ensure that he was kept well warmed. The upholstery of the furniture reflected the wall hangings 'of black and olive colloured Damask hangings wt a scarlet fringe wt silver and black edging'. Here the Duke would turn to his walnut writing cabinets to work on his papers. Charles II conducted dealings with his ministers in his closet or cabinet, hence the modern use of the term for the chief ministers of a government.

The Duchess's Closet (*right*) was furnished in dark mohair bordered with flowered silk with purple and gold fringe, and this scheme has been reconstructed. A late seventeenth-century inventory lists the lacquered eastern-style furniture that she kept here, including 'One Japan Box for sweetmeats and tea'. With Charles II's marriage to the Portuguese princess, Catherine of Braganza, tea-drinking had become the fashion at the Stuart court. [AVE]

The state apartments situated on the first floor at HAM HOUSE were prepared in 1673 for the visit of Catherine of Braganza. The suite of rooms followed the conventional order – antechamber, bedchamber and closet. The Queen's Bedchamber has been much altered, but her closet survives almost unchanged (*left*). Although small, it was very richly decorated, with alternative sets of hangings for summer and winter. For summer there was Chinese silk with painted figures, and for winter, crimson and gold-brocaded satin, bordered with green and gold striped silk. The latter still survives, along with a beautifully decorated scagliola fireplace, and a fine parquet floor. The alcove was probably intended to contain a couch or day-bed, and is now furnished with an upholstered armchair with an adjustable back, described in the inventory of 1679 as a sleeping chair. [AVE]

BENINGBROUGH HALL, like Ham, has a series of apartments with accompanying closets. The grandest of these is the state apartment which consists of withdrawing room, bedchamber, closet and dressing room. These were intended not just as private rooms, but also for ceremonial visits by other guests where a strict form of hierarchy was observed: the more important you were, the further you could proceed into the apartment.

Right: The enfilade, the vista from the state dressing room, looking through the bedchamber to the withdrawing room beyond. [AVE]

DYRHAM PARK in Gloucestershire was built between 1692 and 1704 by William Blaythwayt, who never 'pretended to any fortune', but worked his way up to become Secretary of State to William III. Two of the beds that he brought to the house survive as excellent examples of the very ornate baroque style of Daniel Marot, the King's favourite designer.

In the Queen Anne Room is the state bed made for the house *c.*1704, with crimson and yellow velvet hangings and an interior of sprigged satin (*left*). A suite of walnut chairs has matching covers.

Around the top of the bed runs a rail from which case curtains were hung. The original case curtains were of red cheney, an inexpensive light woollen fabric which would be drawn to keep light and dust from the valuable velvets. [AVE]

Indian and Chinese fabrics and furniture became very fashionable in the seventeenth century, boosted by the trading activities of the East India Company. To have a bedchamber decorated in the Chinese style was particularly popular, and Gervase Jackson-Stops in *The English Country House: A Grand Tour* suggests that 'exotic fantasies may have been considered a suitable accompaniment to the world of dreams'.

When John Meller, a wealthy lawyer, was furnishing his house at ERDDIG in North Wales, he went for the oriental style for his best bedchamber (*right*). In 1720 a carved and gilded bedstead was ordered from the London furniture maker, John Belchier. The hangings and coverlet were originally white, but have now aged to a rich ivory. They are of silk embroidered in the Chinese manner, but known as 'Indian needlework'. Belchier was also commissioned to provide the bedroom furniture, including a scarlet japanned bureau and a set of green japanned chairs and stools.

Originally the best bedchamber was on the ground floor, but by the 1770s it was unusual for bedrooms to be located there, so John Meller's splendid bed and furnishings were moved upstairs, into a room appropriately hung with Chinese hand-painted wallpaper. [AVE]

At SALTRAM in Devon the Parker family had such a taste for chinoiserie that the house contains several rooms with Chinese wallpaper and furnishings. The Chinese Chippendale Bedroom was put together following incendiary damage during the second world war, but provides a splendid re-creation of the mid-eighteenth century (*left*). The walls are hung with painted cotton hangings, with Chinese mirror paintings in English Rococo frames. The bed is very similar in style to one reproduced by Thomas Chippendale in his famous *Gentleman and Cabinet-maker's Director* of 1754.

Above: A detail of another Chinese mirror painting, in the Mirror Room at Saltram. Again, it is contained within an eighteenth-century English giltwood frame with exuberant and exotic decoration in the Rococo style. [AVE]

The taste in chinoiserie for bedrooms continued right through the century and beyond. English cotton manufacturers began to imitate the hand-painted oriental silks, producing not only chintzes with figurative oriental designs, but also developing the floral motifs that still decorate many modern bedrooms.

RECTE ET SUAVITER

Robert Adam's circuit of public rooms in the central block at KEDLESTON contains a state bedroom, dressing room and wardrobe. They lie between the saloon and the dining room, which seems an odd location, but Adam wished to establish a formal, rather old-fashioned style of living at Kedleston, reflecting perhaps the antiquity of the Curzon family, who could trace their ancestors back to the Norman Conquest. The drawing room, which would be expected to 'withdraw' from the bedroom and which has the same colour scheme of blue damask, is situated across the Marble Hall.

The state bedroom and dressing room in their decoration are far from old-fashioned: a combination of the flamboyant Rococo style in the furnishings, such as the state bed; and the severe neo-classical style in the architectural surround. The state bed is made of cedar wood, carved and gilded to give the effect of palm trees with writhing roots. The palm theme extends to all the furnishings in the state bedroom and dressing room, where the gilt mirrors and candlestands are decorated with fronds to represent an allegory of fertility and of hospitality (*above*). [NM]

Right: The Crimson Bedroom at BASILDON PARK in Berkshire, built by the architect John Carr in the 1770s for fellow Yorkshireman Sir Francis Sykes, a nabob who had made his fortune in the East India Company. A sketch plan of the house made in 1840 shows two distinct ranges of bedrooms: the family side and the Regent's side. The family rooms were reached by side stairs, while the Regent's side – a reference to the visit to Basildon of the Prince Regent in 1813 – was approached by the great staircase. The Crimson Bedroom is one of the family rooms, and takes its name from the magnificent early nineteenth-century bed and its accompanying furnishings and suite of furniture. These were brought to the house in 1953 by Lord and Lady Iliffe, but show the style of furnishings of the period.

Nineteenth-century dressing rooms were often used not only for dressing but bathing too. Although fitted bathrooms with hot and cold water were introduced into country houses from the 1820s, many owners preferred the luxury of taking their bath in front of a fire in their dressing room or bedroom. *Left*: Captain Shelton's dressing room at THE ARGORY, with its bath tub and hot water cans, plus the stone hot water bottle for warming the bed. In the background is the triangular stand, known as a toiletry, for basins and ewers for hand washing. [AVE]

Left: The Owl Bedroom at CRAGSIDE, designed by the architect Norman Shaw for the visit of the Prince and Princess of Wales in 1884. The tester or ceiling of the bedstead has been cut down to produce the half-tester, the fashion in the nineteenth century. In this case the bed is made of South American black walnut. The Prince and Princess were provided with a plumbed-in washstand in the bedroom itself, plus a second washstand and a sunken bath in the adjoining dressing room. These facilities were unusually elaborate, for Lord Armstrong was always technologically ahead of his times. [AVE]

By this period the bedchamber, which had spent centuries wandering from the ground floor to the upper levels according to dictates of fashion and status, was almost always located upstairs. The grand vista of state apartments had given way to the privacy of corridors, with bedrooms leading off. Country-house weekends became a feature of the later nineteenth century, which led to a proliferation of bedrooms to accommodate all the guests. At Blickling a series of bedrooms known as the Lothian Row were provided on the top floor, while at Waddesdon Manor in Buckinghamshire a Bachelors' Wing was built by Baron Ferdinand de Rothschild.

The Prince of Wales was a fervent connoisseur of country-house weekends. In the King's Bedroom at PENRHYN CASTLE in North Wales is the brass bed installed for his visit in 1894 (*right*). The fashion for metal bedsteads took off after the Great Exhibition of 1851 – and a huge range was produced, from plain single beds for institutions and servants' quarters, to this very ornate version with its bedposts and tester. [AVE]

Rooms for Contemplation

Medieval castles and manor houses almost always had chapels with resident chaplains. Great households, like that of Henry Percy, 5th Earl of Northumberland at Petworth in the early sixteenth century had a whole hierarchy of chapel staff from the dean to child singers. After the Reformation, however, chapels were only to be found in larger houses, or where there was a particular reason for one. The master of the house might conduct prayers, while formal services were held in the parish church which was often located nearby.

In the sixteenth century those who owned books kept them in their chambers, usually in boxes. Bess of Hardwick's inventory lists six books kept in a coffer in her very overcrowded bedchamber. Henry Percy, 9th Earl of Northumberland had a substantial collection of books, some of which are still at Petworth, their bindings marked with the Percy crescent. Rooms set aside for books make their appearance in the seventeenth century for men of taste and learning known as virtuosi. The Duke of Lauderdale had a library installed at Ham House in the 1670s. Although his actual books have gone, the room is now furnished with another collection from a slightly later period. On the other side of the long gallery is the Green Closet, where he housed his collection of miniature paintings and rare curiosities.

Libraries became an accepted part of the country house in the eighteenth century, often placed in one pavilion with the chapel in the other. This was the age of reason, when a knowledge of literature and the arts was an important way of displaying your social status. But by the nineteenth century the library has often become a general living room rather than a place of silent contemplation: Robert Kerr describes it as 'rather a kind of morning room for gentlemen than anything else'.

The chapel at COTEHELE was built towards the end of the fifteenth century, with an oak rood screen separating the chancel and altar from the rest of the room, as in most parish churches of the period. The chapel lies between the main courtyard of the house – the Hall Court – and the Retainers' Court: the family could view it from squints in their solar and the Priest's Room, while servants might look in through the broad west window.

In the south-west corner of the chapel is a clock installed by Sir Richard Edgcumbe in the 1480s. It is the earliest domestic clock in England, unaltered and in its original position. There are no hands but a shaft connects to the belfry above, so that one bell might toll to summon the household to services, and a second to strike the hours. [AVE]

BADDESLEY CLINTON'S chapel has a long and fascinating religious history. Probably the great chamber of the medieval owners of Baddesley, it was used as a chapel in the 1590s when the house was let by Henry Ferrers and became a refuge for Jesuit priests (*right*). Families who held to the Catholic faith in Elizabethan England were known as recusants, incurring fines for non-attendance at church and being barred from public office. Ferrers himself was a devout Catholic though he never registered as a recusant. For Roman Catholic priests caught in England the penalty was a terrible death, so that the chapel at Baddesley served both as their place of worship and bedroom: in times of peril they would shelter in hiding places known as 'priest's holes'.

In the nineteenth century Baddesley Clinton was home to four extraordinary people known as 'the Quartet': Marmion Ferrers, his artist wife, Rebecca Dulcibella Orpen, her aunt, Lady Chatterton, and her husband, Edward Dering. They loved the antiquity of the house and did much to re-create its medieval atmosphere. When Lady Chatterton converted to Catholicism in 1875, the chapel and its accompanying sacristy (*left*) were refurbished in the style to be seen today. [AVE]

The fine baroque chapel at WIMPOLE HALL was created in the 1720s for Lord Harley, even though the parish church lay just a few yards away. It was designed by James Gibbs, with *trompe-l'oeil* painting by Sir James Thornhill. To the left can be seen two of the 'statues' of Doctors of the Church, while a great canvas showing the *Adoration of the Magi* hangs at the east end. The open, rectangular layout of the chapel at Wimpole would have been ideal for performances by Lord Harley's private orchestra under their music master, Dr Tudway.

Originally the servants sat in box pews facing the altar, but this arrangement was altered later in the eighteenth century to the college chapel style, with rows of stalls facing each other. The photograph is taken from the family pew at the west end. In the sixteenth century the master and his family might worship in the private closet adjoining their chambers, but the idea of a family closet or pew overlooking the chapel became a common feature of seventeenth-century country-house chapels. The service books are all that remain of Harley's great collection at Wimpole.

Above: A detail of one of Thornhill's *putto* on the coving supporting the ceiling. [AVE]

The guidebook to WIMPOLE HALL describes it as the embodiment of 'Toryism defiant'. Robert Harley, 1st Earl of Oxford, leader of the Tory party, fell spectacularly from grace in the troubled political times at the death of Queen Anne and the subsequent Hanoverian succession. Harley's son Edward, inheriting the title and estates in 1724, resolved to make Wimpole a centre of art and learning. His father had been one of the greatest book collectors of his day; his son took over the mantle, amassing a collection of 8,000 volumes of manuscripts, 50,000 printed books, over 350,000 pamphlets, 41,000 prints and dozens of albums of drawings.

To house the greater part of this collection Edward Harley commissioned James Gibbs to build the library at Wimpole. Within the magnificent space of the double cube he installed the arcaded bookcases, all that remains in this room to remind us of Harley's collection. By 1740 he was bankrupt and his estates put up for sale, and Wimpole was bought by the Whig Lord Chancellor, 1st Earl of Hardwicke. So heavy was the blow that by June 1741 Harley was dead. His widow sold the vast book collection for only £13,000, while the manuscripts were bought for the nation for £10,000 and formed the foundation of the British Library. His bookcases, meanwhile, were used to store the fine books of Lord Hardwicke and his descendants. [AVE]

The library at DUNHAM MASSEY was installed
in the 1730s, yet looks old-fashioned in comparison
with Harley's interior at Wimpole: indeed it actually
looks more like a seventeenth-century country-house
library. Fitted oak shelves are lined with the books
belonging to George Booth, 2nd Earl of Warrington,
a man of conservative tastes, whose principal interests
lay in religious literature, politics, genealogy and
history.

The library still has many of its eighteenth-
century furnishings including an orrery with its full
constellation of the sun and the six planets then
known, and a companion armillary sphere, dating
from about 1730 and made by Thomas Wright, the
King's instrument maker. They have their original
oak stands and covers. The Earl's telescope stands
on one of the window sills. Above the fireplace is a
carving of the Crucifixion by the young Grinling
Gibbons, based on the painting by Tintoretto. In
his diary John Evelyn describes how he came upon
Gibbons at work on it in a 'solitary thatched house
in a field' in Deptford. It was probably bought by
the 2nd Earl in the 1680s and an inventory of 1758
places it in its present position. [AVE]

In 1738 William Windham II of FELBRIGG HALL in Norfolk set off for the Continent with his tutor, Benjamin Stillingfleet. Over the next four years they travelled in Switzerland, Italy and the Low Countries, collecting pictures and books all the while. When William inherited Felbrigg in 1749, he commissioned the architect James Paine to refashion the interior, including a cabinet for the display of his pictures, and a library for his books.

The cabinet (*right*) houses an amazingly complete survival of an eighteenth-century collection made on the Grand Tour. Windham was present at the picture hang, to ensure that a special place was given to six large oil paintings and twenty-six gouaches of Rome and its environs by Giovanni Battista Busiri. [NM]

For the library (*left*) Windham decided to go for the Gothick look with little pinnacles atop the bookshelves. The core of the book collection is Windham's, reflecting his interests in architecture, natural history and military drill as well as wood-turning and fireworks which were personal hobbies. William Windham III was also a great bibliophile, adding to his father's collection and creating a sitting room next door where he would sleep in a tent bed so that he could always be near his library. [NM]

Not only does WIMPOLE have a magnificent library (pp.130–1), but also an elegant Book Room (*right*), designed by Sir John Soane in 1806 to accommodate the 3rd Earl of Hardwicke's books. Arches decorated with plaster *paterae* or rosettes spring from the projecting bookcases. A black basalt bust of David Garrick stands on a circular table (*see back cover*), while plaster urns made to look like black Wedgwood basalt – very fashionable library accoutrements for the period – stand atop each bookcase. [AVE]

When Robert Adam's original library at SALTRAM was turned into a dining room (p.92) in 1778, the Parkers' book collection was housed in the first section of the room shown far right. The 1st Lord Boringdon's sister wrote: 'The Library is wonderfully improved and the difference of the size is greater than I supposed it would be. The bookcases being mahogany will look dark, I think, when they grow old, but at present they look very well indeed, and the room is extremely pretty'. But as the collection of books grew, and the status of having a library also rose, so the room needed to be enlarged. In 1819 a hole was knocked through to the drawing room and a screen of four scagliola pillars installed. Although this is a serious library, with a fine collection, including many prints and drawings of Old Masters, the room has a social feel about it rather than that of a place set aside for silent study. [AVE]

The novelist Maria Edgeworth, visiting Bowood in Wiltshire in 1818, wrote of the library, 'tho' magnificent is a most comfortable habitable looking room ... after breakfast this day - groups round various tables – books and prints – and Lord Grenville shaking his leg and reading was silent and I suppose, happy.'

Above: The Print Room at BLICKLING. Originally a bedroom, by 1793 it was known as the Copperplate Room. Lord Buckinghamshire had adopted the fashion for pasting on the walls engravings with decorative borders as though they were framed paintings. Altogether there are fifty-two prints including several by Piranesi and others engraved after works by Rubens, Raphael, Claude, Reynolds and Angelica Kauffman. [NM]

Right: The library at POLESDEN LACEY – a room for contemplation has definitely become a room for living. It was, apparently, Mrs Greville's favourite room. In the centre is a large nineteenth-century mahogany writing table, covered in framed photographs of Mrs Greville's guests 'all with signed inscriptions testifying to their friendship for this popular hostess', and a whole series of vases of flowers in the style of the period. [AVE]

The chapel at LYME PARK has probably occupied its current space since the late sixteenth century, but has been altered over the years to fit changing circumstances. The grand family pew to the right was introduced by Richard Legh c.1680, although the carpentry dates from the 1730s. Lewis Wyatt placed Gothick tracery in front of the sash windows in the early nineteenth century. By 1900 the chapel was rarely used. Phyllis Sandeman, in her delightful memoir of Lyme at that time, *Treasure on Earth*, recalls it as 'a storing place for surplus furniture, chairs, and rout seats for dancers and Fraulein's [the governess's] bicycle'. Since 1950 the chapel has been reconsecrated. [AVE]

SAVE, LORD, AND HEAR US, O KING OF HEAVEN, WHEN WE CALL UPON THEE.

As at Lyme, the chapel at ERDDIG has changed over the centuries. Built by John Meller in the 1720s, its current arrangement reflects its appearance at the beginning of the twentieth century. A biblical text running just below the ceiling was cut out by Philip Yorke II in 1909 with the assistance of his elder son. Philip's first wife had left him shortly after their honeymoon and it was not until her death twenty-two years later that he was free to marry again. The arrival of his two sons, Simon in 1903 and Philip in 1905, must have seemed like a miracle, and the frieze was put up in celebration. [AVE]

Andreas von Einsiedel

Andreas was born and educated in Germany. In 1974 he came to London to take a degree in Photographic Arts at the Polytechnic of Central London and, after graduating, worked as an assistant to one of Germany's leading commercial photographers in Hamburg. In 1979 he decided to marry and to settle in the UK and, thinking it might be a good idea to try something else in life, worked on a sheep farm in the Scottish Highlands. But the following year he returned to London and to photography, assisting Norman Gold with his car images. He loved the technical aspects of this type of work, the large format cameras, controlled lighting and discipline it entailed. In May 1981 he became a freelance photographer, initially concentrating on studio-based still-lifes for advertising.

The launch of *World of Interiors* in 1981 proved a major influence – for him it blew all other home/decorating magazines out of the water, and revealed interior photography as a discipline in its own right. Indeed, *World of Interiors* continues to inspire him, setting the standards he aspires to. Andreas's first interiors were sold to *House & Garden*, although it took several years to graduate to being commissioned. Once this happened, he became one of their regular photographers, producing an enormous amount of work over the next five years. Now his name is not tied to any one magazine, and he works for a wide variety of interior magazines all over the world. He has also been the principal photographer for several books, from Malcolm Hillier's *Dried Flower Arranging* to *Table Chic* by the interior designer Kelly Hoppen. For the National Trust's *Art of Dress* he photographed some of the magnificent costumes from the Killerton and Snowshill collections in a studio setting.

For him, the most important aspect of interior photography is how the light is handled. He relishes the English light, even the grey and overcast days which may seem unpromising but provide the perfect illumination for many interiors. A very long exposure, a minute or more, often adds an indefinable quality to the images. When lighting interiors, artificial light must be used with discretion, playing a supporting role to the main natural source, filling in shadows and reducing contrast. The impression that the space has been lit naturally should be retained.

He now works almost exclusively on 120 film. Editorial work is shot on Hasselblad, which yields square originals. For the kind of interiors required by the National Trust he often uses 6 x 7 and 6 x 9 formats, with a Linhof Technikardan, a wonderful example of German camera engineering. He uses almost exclusively Kodak materials for interiors: Kodak EPP and EPN. EPP is used for 95 per cent of his work, as it copes brilliantly with mixed lighting, very long exposures, and is not too contrasty. EPN is used when the exact colour rendition of materials and textiles is important, or when he requires a slightly cooler feel to the overall colour balance.

Andreas has worked for the National Trust for about ten years, since the then Photographic Manager of the Library, Diana Lanham, instigated a drive for higher quality, more contemporary, and hence more commercial photography. He has loved the assignments given him, which are in the main seasonal, either just before the houses open to the public in spring, or once they have closed down for the winter. The privilege of having the house virtually to himself, with unrestricted access is immeasurable, for rooms lose their museum atmosphere in these circumstances. He enjoys the effect of changing light on a particular room, perhaps coming back and photographing it again under completely different lighting conditions.

Nadia was born in London and studied for a degree in graphic design and photography at Exeter College of Art and Design. Her thesis on 'Surrealism in Japanese Advertising Photography' led to her introduction to a leading Japanese fashion photographer, Akira Kobayashi, and an offer to be his assistant in London. His personal encouragement to pursue her interest in the great photographers working on the west coast of America, such as Ansel Adams and Bret Weston, enabled her to build up a large portfolio following her travels there. The attraction of interesting places and their inhabitants, reinforced by the early inspiration of her architect father, drove her ambition to create and record still-life images on location rather than in the studio.

The launch of *World of Interiors* was a revelation. She began working for them in 1987 – her first commissioned interior shoot. Subsequently she moved between editorial clients, book publishers, design groups and corporate work in the UK and overseas. These commissions broadened her scope and were put to good use when she began working for the National Trust in the winter of 1992, photographing the interior of Felbrigg Hall, Norfolk. The challenge then and for all Trust commissions is to capture the intrinsic atmosphere of the property and translate this into memorable images for successful marketing.

For her interior work she uses Sinar 5 x 4, Mamiya 6 x 7 or 6 x 6 Hasselblad and Kodak EPP 120 film. She believes it is the natural light that is all important. On arrival at a National Trust property Nadia does a recce of the house, assessing how the natural light will work, using Polaroids to get the best angles and making notes. Her aim is to 'paint with light', mixing flash light with the available daylight. For instance when shooting the Marble Hall at Kedleston Hall in Derbyshire, the challenge was to achieve the right light balance, since the vast columned room (p.23) is top-lit by a small dome. The scenario was rather like lighting a football pitch with a torch! However, a combination of carefully concealed flash lights together with a very long timed exposure created the desired effect. Working out where to hide the necessary flash lights is one of the practicalities of shooting historic interiors: they must not reflect off large mirrors, they must be kept away from walls for safety reasons, they must be rigged onto high stands to highlight the ceilings, and they must not flare off any oil paintings adorning the walls.

For Nadia an important part of the picture's message is to give an insight into the lives of earlier inhabitants. These may be depicted as small still-life details such as a cabinet of glassware, fragile textiles, or valuable silver, often impossible to put on public display, but which nevertheless convey a sense of history worthy of recording.

Index